14.95

MAR 1 9 1998

BEDBUGS IN OUR HOUSE

Cockchafer beetle
scientific name: Melolontha melolontha

American cockroaches
scientific name: Periplaneta americana

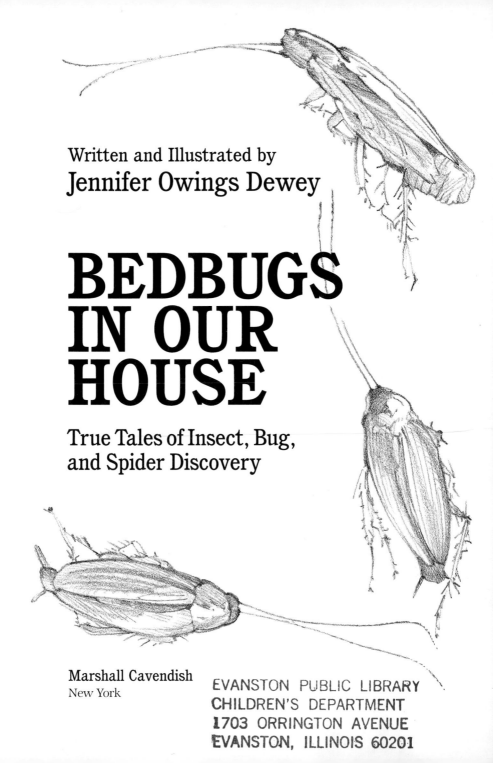

Written and Illustrated by
Jennifer Owings Dewey

BEDBUGS IN OUR HOUSE

True Tales of Insect, Bug,
and Spider Discovery

Marshall Cavendish
New York

THIS BOOK IS FOR DORY, MY FRIEND AND PEN PAL

Text and illustrations copyright © 1997 by Jennifer Owings Dewey
All rights reserved.
Marshall Cavendish, 99 White Plains Road, Tarrytown, New York 10591
The text of this book is set in 12 point Zapf International Light
The illustrations are rendered in pencil
Printed in the United States of America   First edition   6 5 4 3 2 1

Library of Congress Cataloging-in-Publication Data
Dewey, Jennifer Owings.
Bedbugs in our house : true tales of insect, bug, and spider discovery /
written and illustrated by Jennifer Owings Dewey. — 1st ed.
p.   cm.   Includes index.
Summary: The author presents interesting facts about insects, bugs, and
spiders in chapters that describe her own experiences living with and
studying these creatures when she was a child.
ISBN 0-7614-5006-8
1. Insects—Juvenile Literature. [1. Insects. 2. Spiders.] I. Title.
QL467.2.D48   1997 595.7—dc21   97-12787   CIP   AC

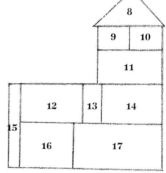

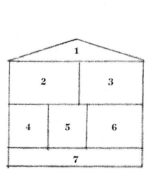

Jacket illustration:

1. thrip *(Thysanoptera)*

2. Pennsylvania firefly
     (photuris Pennsylvania)

3. Eastern tent caterpillar (male)
     (Malacosoma americanum)

4. common garden spider
     (Argiope)

5. cornfield ant *(Lasis niger)*

6. clover leafhopper
     (Aceratagallia sanguinolenta)

7. larva of lacewing
     (Corychucha marmorata)

8. red-velvet mite *(Thrombididae)*

9. wood louse (pill bug or sow bug)
     (Oniscoidea)

10. cabbage butterfly eggs
      (Pieris rapae)

11. Eastern net wing *(Lycus luteralis)*

12. dog flea *(Ctenocephalides canis)*

13. glowworm
      (Microphotus angustus)

14. human bedbug
      (Cimex lectularius)

15. aquatic fly larva *(Stratiomyia)*

16. two-spotted lady beetle
      (Adalia bipunctata)

17. violet sawfly
      (Ametastegia pallipes)

CONTENTS

CLASSES OF INSECTS

Protura

Primitive insects with no eyes, antennae, or wings. These animals have twelve segments to their bodies and live in soil.

Collembola

Small insects with no wings and long legs they can use for leaping. Their bodies have six segments and most live in soil.

Thysanura

Insects with soft, flat bodies and no pigment, or color. Called bristletails, these insects are short-legged but fast.

Ephemeroptera

Mayflies, the most primitive winged insects, have short antennae on their heads. The nymph lives in fast-flowing water.

Odonata

Dragonflies, insects with two pairs of wings and biting mouth-parts. Dragonflies have slim legs and short antennae, and their eyes nearly cover their heads. The nymph stage lives in water.

Plecoptera

Stone flies are insects found close to water. They are flat, with large wings, and have biting mouthparts. The larvae live in water and eat plants, although some are carnivores, or meat eaters.

Orthoptera

All insects with agility in movement belong to this class, including grasshoppers, crickets, mantises, and cockroaches. Wing shapes vary, and some species, usually females only, are wingless.

Dermaptera

Earwigs, insects with biting mouthparts, long antennae, and pincers on their back ends, are in this class. These animals live on rotting plants.

Psocoptera

Lice belong to this class, small insects with fairly long antennae and biting mouthparts. There are several kinds of lice, from those that eat books to those preferring bark or garbage, and even some that feed on glue.

Hemiptera

These are the true bugs, insects with distinctive mouthparts and wings that differ from other insects. The head has a snout used for piercing and sucking. A bug's wings are usually hard and held flat against the body. Many bugs are parasites or predators. A large number of true bugs are water dwellers.

Neuroptera

This class includes lacewings and dobsonflies, snakeflies and alderflies. These insects undergo complete metamorphosis. They have huge wings with a dense network of veins.

Trichoptera

Caddis flies, with aquatic larvae, are in this class of insects. The antennae are long and slender, as are the legs. Caddis flies in larval forms build cases to protect their soft bodies, tiny "houses" made of leaf bits, pebbles, mud, and often saliva or silk produced in the larva's insides.

Lepidoptera

In this class are the butterflies and moths, insects that undergo complete metamorphosis, a developmental change in form or structure. All have big, compound eyes (made up of many separate visual units), four wings, and colored scales. Most have sucking mouthparts; only the most primitive have biting mouthparts.

Diptera

These are the true flies, insects with two wings and compound eyes. Mosquitos are in this class. Their mouthparts may be the lapping type, such as in houseflies, or the sucking kind, as in mosquitos and horseflies.

Siphonaptera

Fleas are in this class of insects. These insects have especially long legs and can leap great distances. The larvae have no legs. Fleas are parasites that live on a host's skin and feed on meals of blood.

Coleoptera

The largest class of insects on earth are the beetles. Their forewings are hard, and their heads have biting mouthparts, a pair of antennae, and compound eyes. Beetles are not great fliers. Their larvae live on land and in freshwater environments. Beetles consume food in a variety of ways. Many beetles are decomposers, eating the droppings of other animals.

Homoptera

This class consists of leafhoppers, cicadas, and aphids. There is disagreement among scientists as to whether or not this class of insects ought to be lumped together with the true bugs. They are, in fact, similar to true bugs in many respects, including their sucking mouthparts.

Hymenoptera

Bees, ants, and wasps belong to this class of insects. These insects have four wings, long legs, and compound eyes. Their mouthparts may be the lapping, sucking, or biting kind.

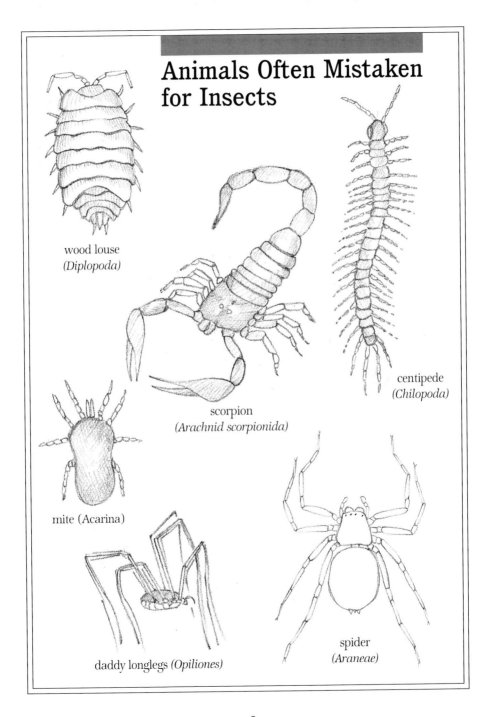

Animals Often Mistaken for Insects

wood louse
(Diplopoda)

scorpion
(Arachnid scorpionida)

centipede
(Chilopoda)

mite (Acarina)

daddy longlegs *(Opiliones)*

spider
(Araneae)

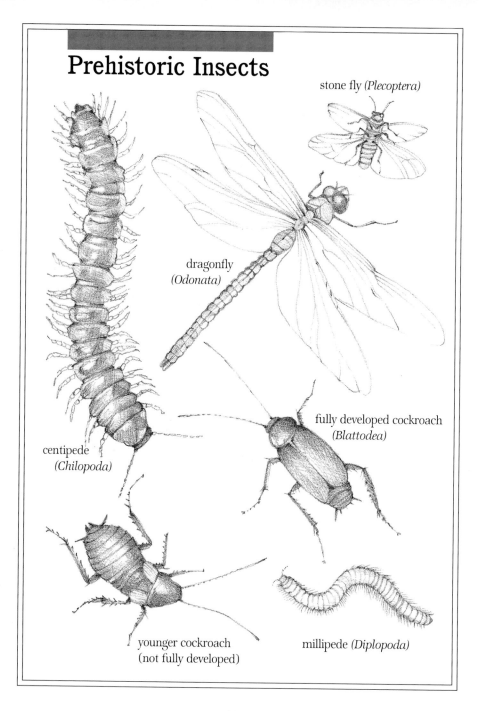

Prehistoric Insects

stone fly *(Plecoptera)*

dragonfly
(Odonata)

fully developed cockroach
(Blattodea)

centipede
(Chilopoda)

younger cockroach
(not fully developed)

millipede *(Diplopoda)*

Introduction

A FLY IN AN AMBER TOMB

primitive stone fly in amber   *scientific name: Plecoptera*

I was six years old when my grandfather came from Chicago to visit us. He brought presents for all the children. Mine was the best.

It was a marble-sized, honey-colored amber bead with an insect— a fly—trapped inside.

"The fly lived fifty million years ago," my grandfather told me. "How do you suppose it ended up in that bead?"

My fascination with insects and spiders had already led me to many discoveries, but this question was too hard for me to answer.

"How?" I asked. "Do you know?"

"Yes," my grandfather said. "And I'd be happy to tell you about it."

He filled my head with insect history. I learned that insects first appeared on earth four hundred million years ago, the descendants of sea animals with segmented bodies.

At first no insects flew. After one hundred million years passed, some insects took to the air, humming, buzzing, and beating their wings.

Flying insects landed on trees to rest or to look for food. Some became stuck in gummy resin, or sap, oozing from cuts in the bark. When the sap hardened, the insects were trapped and preserved for eternity.

Heat, pressure, and age changed the sap into amber, a semi-precious stone. People polish lumps of amber, smoothing and rounding them into beads.

I held my bead in my hand and wondered what would happen if I broke it in two. Would I see the ancient fly's leg more clearly? Or the veins in its tiny wings?

"You would see only dust," my grandfather said. "The fly is a ghost of itself, not a real fly."

I curled my fingers closely around the bead and told my grandfather it was a treasure I would keep always. He smiled, pleased that what he had given me meant so much.

I hold the bead now and then to remind myself of a time when the mysteries of insect lives first captured my imagination.

fruit fly
(*Tephritidae*)

12

One

BEDBUGS IN OUR HOUSE?

bedbug   *scientific name: Cimex lectularius*

On a summer morning when I was nine, I came to the breakfast table scratching a dozen or so small red bites that had appeared on my body during the night. The bites were mostly on my stomach, but a few were on the soft flesh of my upper arms.

My father quickly noticed my energetic scratching. "What's the matter with you?" he asked. "Why are you scratching like that?"

"It's nothing. Just some bites."

"Let me see," my mother said, looking concerned.

I went to my mother and lifted my tee-shirt, exposing an array of tiny, inflamed bumps.

"Bedbugs," my mother declared.

"Bedbugs? In our house? Impossible," my father said in disbelief. "Come here," he ordered. "Let me see those bites."

My mother was right; the bites had been inflicted by bedbugs. They had occurred while I slept soundly in my bed.

"Who have you been playing with?" my father angrily demanded to know. "And where?"

I thought it a strange question.

"With my sisters and my brother. With my usual friends."

My father was unhappy with my answer. In fact, it made him even angrier.

"You're not supposed to have bedbug bites," he said, his face flushed.

"Why not? I've been bitten by plenty of things since I was born, and you never minded before. What's so bad about bedbugs?"

My father had the idea "normal" people, such as we, did not get **infested** (in-FEST-ed) *(his word)* with bedbugs. "We're clean," he said with emphasis. "Only dirty people in filthy houses have **vermin** (VERM-in) in their beds." I could see he was prejudiced against our neighbors.

My father insisted the solution to our problem was to call the fumigators. "**Fumigating** (FEW-muh-gate-ing) means killing with poison gas," he told us. "We'll get rid of those bedbugs and every other bug in this house, as well."

By the time our discussion reached this stage, I knew that bedbugs like hiding in mattresses. "Why not get me a new bed?" I suggested, thinking this a much better idea than poisonous gas. It scared me to think of the rooms of our house cloudy with deadly gases and every insect inhabitant killed, but my objections fell on deaf ears.

The fumigators came, unloading their truck and setting cans of poison on the ground in the front yard. Each can was labeled with a skull and crossbones. The fumigating took two days. We were not allowed inside during this time. We spent our days with friends and slept on the lawn in sleeping bags for two nights. My parents left us in the care of a baby-sitter and went off to town to stay in a motel.

When it was all over and I was permitted back in the house, I was stunned by what I saw. The brick floors looked like war zones with no survivors. The dead were everywhere, on their backs with their legs sticking stiffly up in the air.

14

I helped sweep the bodies into piles in the yard, and I watched as my father sprinkled the piles with barbecue starter fluid and set them afire. Never before had I realized how many creatures live invisibly, and very quietly, side by side with us.

Insects and spiders soon enough took up residence in our house, but we never had bedbugs again.

I knew my father's attitude toward vermin was common, an ancient fear shared by most humans. When I was a kid we had a chant that went this way:

"From ghoulies, to ghosties, to eight-legged beasties, and all other things that go bump in the night, Good Lord deliver us."

Some people have the opposite view of crawly things. They love to examine a beetle's body or figure out how a spider spins a web. If they make a living with their interest, they are called **entomologists** (en-tuh-MALL-uh-jist).

Before the bedbugs bit me, I wanted to be an entomologist, and afterward I wanted this even more. My family couldn't understand, since I was the victim of the bedbugs, how I continued to be fascinated by insects.

I tried to explain, saying their many legs, great speed across the floor, ability to hide, and complete difference from us in every way aroused my curiosity.

My sisters teased me when I took stink bugs on walks, a length of kite string around their middles. My sisters and my little brother loathed my collection of insects and spiders contained in glass jars on a shelf in my room. I told them they needn't come to my room to look, but they came anyway.

I always tried to let my captives go after a few days, not wanting any single one to die in my care. If by chance I awoke in the morning to find that a beetle or spider had died, I planned an elaborate funeral and buried it in a cemetery I'd picked out, a spot of ground in the plum orchard. If the dead insect had been fond of water, I cremated it and floated the ashes across the pond on a leaf.

Taking care of my charges was a big thing for me, and so too were the rituals I invented, when needed, to see them into another realm. It was a realm I could not describe in words, but I knew it existed.

True Bugs

The word *bug* is used loosely to describe any small animal with many legs that has its skeleton on the outside. All bugs are **insects** (IN-sekt), but not all insects are bugs. Insects belong to an animal group called Arthropoda (ar-THROP-uh-duh).

The physical characteristics of Arthropoda are:

- three body sections: head, **abdomen**
  (AB-doe-men), and **thorax** (THOR-aks);
- jointed limbs;
- tough outside skeletons made of **chitin** (KITE-in).

True bugs such as bedbugs have these insect characteristics, but they also have others that place them in a category of their own. For example, bugs usually have wings. But what really makes them different from other insects is their mouths.

A bug's mouth is long, jointed, and shaped like a beak or snout. The mouth has piercing and sucking features. These allow the bug to drain fluids from plants and animals, which is its way of eating.

Bedbugs are **parasites** (PAIR-uh-site). The word was first used by the ancient Greeks to describe "one who eats at another's table." The uninvited parasitic bug pierces the skin of a host—a human or other animal—and sucks blood. The **protein** (PRO-teen) in blood is needed by the bedbug in order for it to grow.

Like most bugs, bedbugs have eyes, but they see poorly. They find their way in the dark—for they are **nocturnal** (nock-TER-nul)—by using long, sensitive **antennae** (an-TEN-ee). Drawn by warmth, they pierce the skin of the host with hollow mouthparts. The blood meal makes them swell up, turning their bodies bright red.

A full-grown bedbug is less than half an inch long. When not filled with blood, the animal is flat, oval, and reddish-brown in color. Young bedbugs, not fully grown, are **translucent** (trans-LOO-cent).

Old age for a bedbug is six months. After mating, an adult female lays her eggs in a hidden place. (Maybe this is why people hate them so. They are good at hiding.) The eggs hatch in a week.

Freshly hatched bedbugs are called **nymphs** (NIMF). A nymph needs a blood meal in order to grow. With each stage of life—and bedbugs have five nymphal stages—a blood meal is needed.

The bedbugs that bit me when I was a child are the kind that suck human or **mammal** (MAM-ul) blood. Bird bugs and bat bugs also exist. As their names suggest, these parasites feed on the blood of birds or bats. While the bedbugs we were warned about as children hide in bedding, sofas, and mattresses, bird and bat bugs live in the nests or the roosts of their hosts.

True bugs can be found in all sorts of habitats, from flower gardens to streams and ponds. Several species of bugs live in the oceans of the world.

Many species of bugs we commonly see are brilliantly colored. This usually means they are disgusting, or even dangerous, for other animals to eat. The poison in the plants these bugs eat is transferred to any **predator** (PRED-uh-tore) that makes the mistake of swallowing them.

There are at least forty-five hundred species of bugs in North America. Whichever species a person chooses to observe, it is certain that fascinating discoveries will be made about how that animal goes about its bug business.

Common Parasites

bedbug *(Cimex lectularius)*

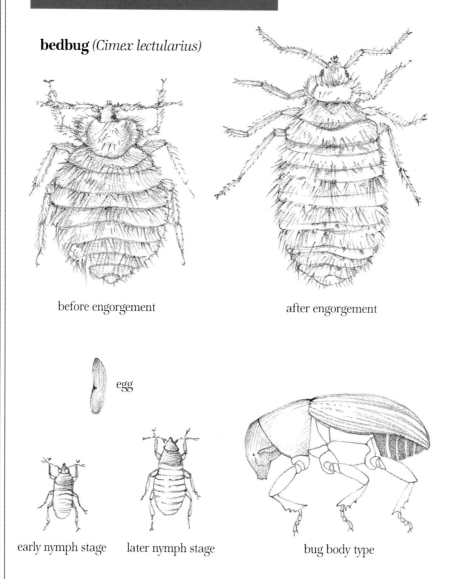

before engorgement

after engorgement

egg

early nymph stage   later nymph stage   bug body type

SUCKING MOUTHPARTS

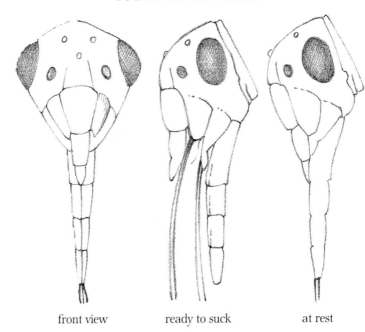

front view   ready to suck   at rest

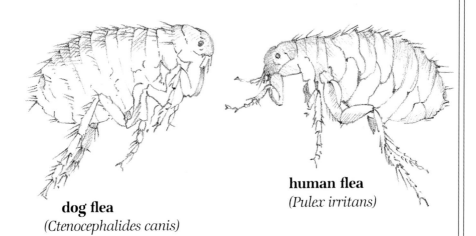

dog flea
(Ctenocephalides canis)

human flea
(Pulex irritans)

Two

EATING EACH OTHER

Carolina mantis   *scientific name: Stagomantis carolina*

I was in the fourth grade when one bright morning Mr. Thomas, our science teacher, stood up to his full six-foot, three-inch height before the class. The kids were hushed into a rare silence. Mr. Thomas held an earthworm in the bony fingers of his right hand. The dangling worm was alive.

For a long moment Mr. Thomas remained still, with his eyes closed. I wondered if he might be saying grace, because he had just told us he intended to eat the worm.

We waited.

Finally he raised his arm, put back his head, opened his mouth wide enough to reveal gold inlays, and dropped the worm onto his tongue.

The worm slid down his skinny throat and, in my mind's eye, I watched it, whole and unchewed, moving along a narrow passage exactly the right shape for swallowing earthworms.

Mr. Thomas gulped once and smiled. The class heaved a sigh of relief. "Time to breathe again," I whispered to myself.

"How come you did that?" a boy asked.

"To impress on you the value of protein," Mr. Thomas answered. "Worms, and many other animals that may disgust you, are high in protein."

A silence followed this statement. We knew Mr. Thomas was leading us to a point of fact he wanted us to understand.

"Are you a **cannibal** (KAN-i-bul)?" he asked a girl in the front row of desks.

"No," she said, smiling nervously. "I'm not."

"Do you eat meat?"

"Yes."

"Then why don't you take advantage of your fellow humans as a meat supply?"

A gentle roll of giggles moved across the room.

"I know," someone said from the back of the room. "Animals don't eat their own kind. It isn't right."

"Depends on the animal," Mr. Thomas said. We could see from his grin that he was pleased. We were beginning to understand the point he was making.

Mr. Thomas went to his overcoat, which was hanging on a hook, and from the pockets pulled out several large white envelopes, their surfaces pierced with tiny holes.

Out of each envelope came an animal which Mr. Thomas dropped, carefully into its own glass baby-food jar. He kept one envelope in reserve.

First came a red-kneed tarantula (ta-RAN-chew-la), followed by a bright green praying mantis (MAN-tiss). Then came a centipede, three inches long, and finally a black widow spider, which Mr. Thomas avoided touching.

"Watch," he said, slipping the black widow into the same jar as the centipede.

We saw a flash battle, one in which the centipede, despite its pincers and many legs, seemed to have no chance at all. Its taffy-colored body curled into a death twist in an instant. The widow's **venom**

(VEN-um) was quick to take effect.

Next Mr. Thomas put the tarantula in with the black widow. The tarantula won this conflict. I guessed the widow was out of venom, having used it all on the centipede. No child uttered a word while the life-and-death encounters went on.

black widow
(Latrodectus mactans)

Mr. Thomas put the leggy mantis in with the hairy tarantula, and in this tangle the mantis won. I decided the tarantula was worn out from its clash with the black widow.

The final drama came when Mr. Thomas gently pulled the mantis from its embrace with the tarantula and placed it in a jar of its own. From the envelope he'd put aside, he brought a second mantis, which he lowered in with the first.

"This one's a female," he whispered.

The two mantises touched gingerly, exploring each other with their front legs and slender antennae. I got the impression these animals "see" with their limbs, although they have excellent eyesight.

In a moment they were in a mating posture. Every child sat in rapt concentration as the female mantis bit off the head of the male and began chewing on it.

"Tooth and claw," Mr. Thomas said softly. "Tooth and claw. To live, every animal must eat," he told our class. "Eating means surviving, and surviving means having a chance to reproduce. Insects have amazing eating habits. They make use of every possible opportunity to fill an empty stomach. They are scavengers or predators or parasites. Insects may eat each other, plants or plant juices, the droppings of other animals, or the microscopic critters living on the droppings."

Once more, as before, Mr. Thomas had the full attention of his students.

"For example, the centipede, now gone to centipede heaven, was fond of dead plant material. The tarantula ate small spiders, perhaps a lizard now and then. Most of you know what spiders eat. We'd be drowning in flies and other kinds of insects if spiders didn't help us out by eating them."

Mr. Thomas went on a while longer, giving us the sort of information we loved. He was never boring.

Eating Habits

Insects leave almost no earthly material alone when it comes to their eating habits. While some are cannibals, a vast number are predators and eat living tissue, meaning other insects. There are more **vegetarians** (vej-eh-TAIR-ee-an) than anything else. Examples of these are fig wasps, which eat only figs; leaf cutters favoring one kind of leaf; or beetles decomposing a tree fallen in the forest. Insects make use of every part of what they eat, wasting nothing.

Insect parasites have different methods for eating. Some burrow into fur or feathers and suck through strawlike mouthparts to get the blood they need. Botfly larvae are parasites, feeding on the blood of their hosts. Ichneumon (ick-nee-YOO-mun) wasps bore holes in wood, drilling with features on their abdomens, to create a safe haven for a developing larva. Many parasitic wasps lay their eggs on caterpillars. By the time the young wasps are ready to be on their own, the caterpillar host is drained dry.

There are a stunning variety of designs in insect mouthparts because the shape a mouth takes is based on what and how the insect eats.

Insects may pass through several forms between their hatching and the time they are fully grown. Their mouthparts and their diets change along the way. Still, even with the variations among insect lifestyles and eating habits, their mouths have a basic structure. As with the beaks of birds, individual features change but the essential organs remain the same.

The mouth begins with a hole where food enters the body. There is an upper lip and a lower one. Jaws brace the hole, and these are what

Insect Mouthparts

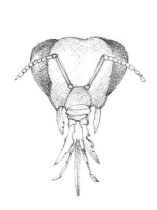

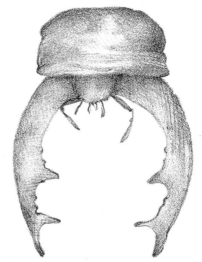

**honeybee
head and mouthparts**
(Apis mellifera)

stag beetle (front view)
(Lucanidae)

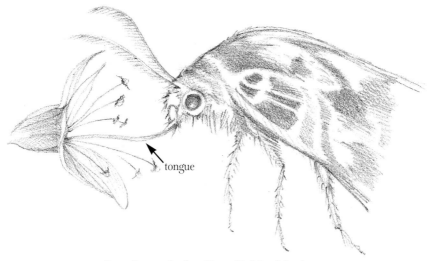

tongue

hawkmoth feeding *(Sphingidae)*

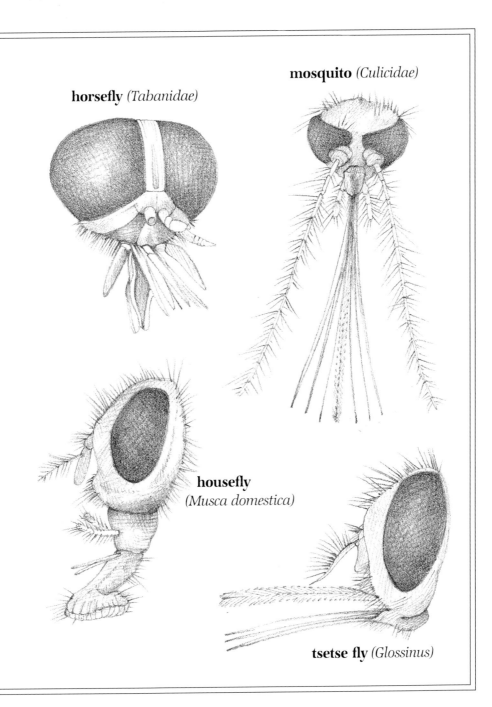

horsefly *(Tabanidae)*

mosquito *(Culicidae)*

housefly *(Musca domestica)*

tsetse fly *(Glossinus)*

25

insects use to chew with. Insects generally do not have teeth. Their **mandibles** (MAN-di-bul) do the cutting and sawing necessary to make food the right size for swallowing.

Sap drinkers, moths, cicadas (si-KAY-duh), and spittlebugs have long, slender tubes on their faces that act as drinking straws. Bugs usually have tubes with segments that are hinged together.

Although spiders are not insects, but instead members of a group called Arachnida (uh-RACK-nid-uh), their mouthparts resemble those of insects. Spiders often use **fangs** to pierce a victim. Venom is injected, and the food source—a fly or grasshopper—is paralyzed. This method allows spiders to have fresh protein around when they need it.

Solitary insects have unsocial habits. They live alone and forage for their food without sharing. The only time they make contact with their own kind is to mate and reproduce.

Social insects—ants, termites, and some bees and wasps—live in organized communities—in nests, mounds, and hives—in which hundreds of thousands of insects divide the labor of staying alive. Food gathering is a task given to certain individuals, but the wealth is shared by all.

Insects suck their food, or sip it or chew it, with an assortment of up to five mouthparts. The success of insects on Earth is surely due in part to their ability to exploit nearly every possible source of food and then find a way to eat it.

Three

THE UNIVERSE IN A MASON JAR

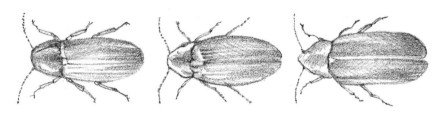

Pennsylvania fireflies   *scientific name: Photuris pennsylvania*

When I was growing up, my best friend was a girl named Martha. Her enthusiasm for searching the woodpile to find black widow spiders was less than my own, but she tagged along. She sat with me in the irrigation ditch, muddy water flowing past, waiting for drowned beetles to show up. Martha helped me organize insect funerals when they were needed, and if something was to be cremated, she nearly always had matches in her pocket.

One of our favorite exploring places was the pond at the bottom of the big cow pasture. A narrow ditch fed the pond on the north and another drained it on the south. All year around, even when ice formed a frigid skin over the pond, we went there to see what we could find, catch, and keep. We took mason jars with us, the lids punched with holes so our captives could breathe.

One especially hot night in August we decided to go down to the pond. Jars in hand, we raced without shoes through the alfalfa field. The sky above was so bright and clear with a zillion stars it made me dizzy. The Milky Way was as plain as day.

We were both ten that summer. For as long as we'd known each other, which was as long as we'd lived, we had discussed things. One question that came up often was, what force, or power, made the Universe work? What held everything together and gave the stars their order? On that August night we wondered again about the answer to this question.

"Look," Martha suddenly exclaimed. "What are those lights in the bushes? They're jumping around in the air."

I saw the lights, but I didn't say anything because I didn't know what they were.

We slowed to a crawl and moved forward in silence so we wouldn't disturb whatever it was that made the flashes. It passed through my mind that the glimmerings were the fires of stars fallen out of the sky.

We were afraid the lights would vanish when we got to the edge of the pond. They stayed and went on flickering. At last we were standing among them, our bare feet up to the ankles in cool water.

I waved my jar in the air, trying to catch one of the bright sparks. The assembly zipped upward, then dropped down, and then rose up again, a pattern of flight repeated over and over.

Unable to capture a light in my jar, I set it down and began reaching into the shimmering cloud with my hands. Martha did the same, and within minutes our jars were alive with darting flames of yellowish-white, each with a blue-green afterglow.

We moved to a spot away from the water and under the willows where we could sit on the damp ground and examine our catches. Martha was as intrigued as I was with what we were seeing.

"What are they?" Martha again wondered aloud. "Are they magic bugs?"

"I think they're fireflies," I said, hesitantly. I'd never seen fireflies before, but it seemed a good guess.

I let one of the captives out of my jar. It did not fly away, but sat perfectly still on the back of my hand. It was a dusky-brown color and less than a quarter-inch long. It had wings. The glimmer it gave off came from the back of its body.

"It looks like a beetle, not a fly," I said, trying to make out the insect's anatomy in the dimness.

"They flicker like Christmas lights," Martha said softly. "The way they go on and off makes me think of the stars. They seem organized in their way of shining. It's like we're seeing the Universe in a mason jar."

I knew what she meant. There appeared to be a plan to the ascending and descending flock of tiny lights, as if they'd been rehearsed.

Half an hour after we'd swooped the little beams of light into our jars, we let them go. We sat in the darkness and watched the main group flashing in unison and dancing as if someone were waving them into action.

Finally the last fire went out and we walked home, firefly flash and starlight in our eyes.

Glowworm is the name given to the larval stages and the wingless females of the firefly. They are pink, and they cluster in the grass, beaming their signals into the darkness.

Fireflies are predators. They eat meat in the form of snails and slugs, and sometimes the larvae of other insects. They attack a victim by injecting it with a toxic fluid that paralyzes it. They suck the insides out. The fireflies Martha and I saw are called Pennsylvania fireflies.

Other insects also emit light. Most of these live in the tropics. A species of springtail, a tiny flealike creature, gives off a greenish glow at mating time. There are several species of moths that make cold light with chemical reactions in their bodies that are like the firefly's. Some of the most astonishing light givers are tropical beetles that glow from head to tail.

Martha and I never figured out what holds the Universe together, but we did learn about one of the myriad fascinating creatures that inhabit it.

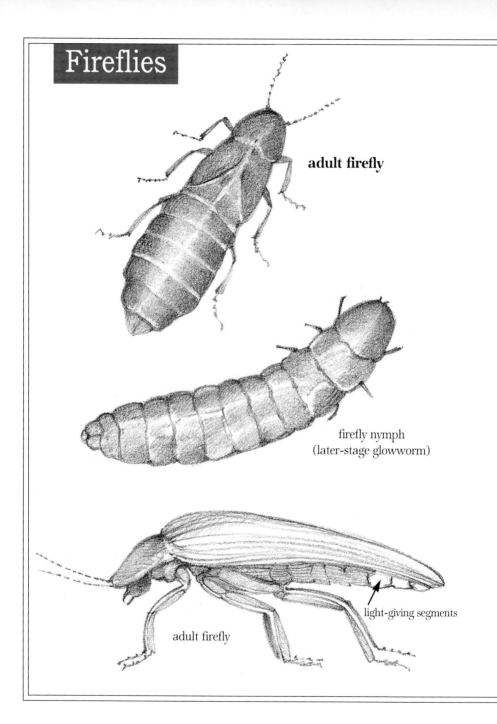

Fireflies

adult firefly

firefly nymph
(later-stage glowworm)

adult firefly

light-giving segments

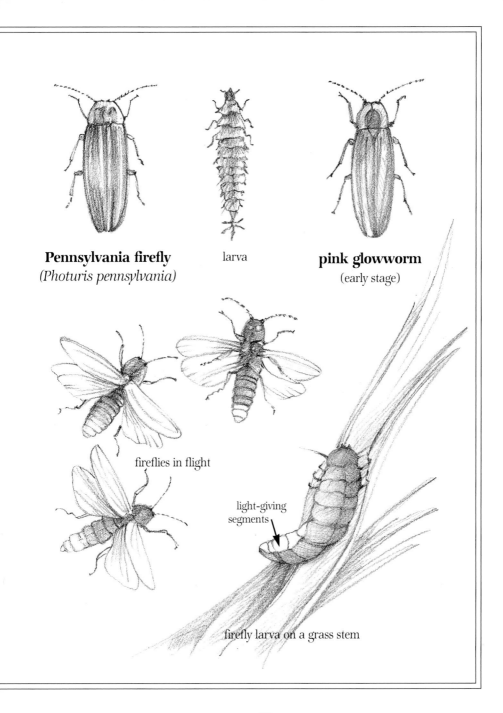

Pennsylvania firefly
(Photuris pennsylvania)

larva

pink glowworm
(early stage)

fireflies in flight

light-giving
segments

firefly larva on a grass stem

Fireflies and Glowworms

On the hottest nights of summer, in July and August, fireflies (also called lightning bugs) make their brilliant displays. The light these animals make is called "cold" because it is produced inside the insect's body when two separate chemicals meet.

The chemicals are called **enzymes** (EN-zime). When it is time for the firefly to mate, these enzymes flow freely into the rear portion of the insect's body and merge. They become "heated" to the glowing point, and thus the light is made.

Males have more light-making segments on their bodies than females, and their flashes tend to be brighter. Male fireflies and some female fireflies have wings and fly about in the air. Females lurk in the grass, waiting to attract the attention of a male, for the entire event of flashing light is for the sake of mating.

Just as fireflies or lightning bugs are neither flies nor bugs, glowworms are not worms. The common names for these larval stages of insects have so often been used that there is no practical way to change them.

Four

BABY BROTHER TRANSFORMED

monarch caterpillar
scientific name: Danaus plexippus

Is it true that most children fantasize about changing a younger sister or brother into a shape that cannot tease or annoy? I ask this because as a child I spent more than a few hours of my time wondering how to change my baby brother into a chair, a rug, or a cupcake someone might accidentally eat. I could think of no way to transform him until I found out about **metamorphosis** (met-uh-MORE-foh-sis).

It was my favorite (and only) science teacher, Mr. Thomas, who introduced me to the concept of metamorphosis. The word means "changes in physical shape and form."

Mr. Thomas liked taking his classes out of doors, to the mountains or the desert, so we could observe nature firsthand. One bright November day he took our class of sixteen third-graders to a meadow in the mountains, a grassy expanse fringed with aspen trees and cut through by a glistening stream of water.

Mr. Thomas instructed us to search for and collect small objects resembling those he held in his hand. He called these bits of leaf and pebble "cases." Some looked like tiny mummies wrapped in green cloth.

"They're not what they seem," he said mysteriously. "Keep what you find. We'll take them back to the zoo." Mr. Thomas was referring to the **terrariums** (teh-RARE-ee-um) in our classroom that were nearly always occupied by captive animals, from spadefoot toads to cockroaches.

We crawled through the thick meadow grass on our hands and knees, plucking away any clinging, dangling, or glued-down piece of something that looked like what Mr. Thomas had shown us. We dug in the black soil, which smelled like birth and death at once, and felt along the stream edges where the mud was cold and slippery.

We searched with eager fingers, and before long our jars were filled to the lids. It was time to go back to town.

On the way, I held my jar in my lap and peered at the contents, an unpromising assortment of round, flat, and oval shapes. I detected no hint of secrets hidden within.

"Insects are not parental," Mr. Thomas said. "Once they have mated and deposited the eggs, attention is given only to protecting those eggs. Few insects hang about to see the eggs hatch, and even fewer assist in the raising of the young. There are exceptions, of course. There are always exceptions in the insect world."

Mr. Thomas rubbed his palms together and smiled. It was easy to see that this was a lecture he enjoyed giving.

"I can give you the example of the female scorpion, a creature who carries her eggs within her body, and when they hatch, carries the little beasts on her back for a stretch of time. And then there are the burying beetles, those all-work-and-no-play insects capable of digging a hole, burying a bird or mouse in it, and creating a full table of food for their growing young to dine on at any time they please."

We listened, as ever, with full attention.

"For any insect that does not hatch looking like a miniature version of its parents, there are stages of growth it must pass through, which are called larval (LAR-vul) stages. Insect **larvae** (LAR-vee) appear in many shapes and sizes. Your collections show this, do they not? A larval insect may be a caterpillar, a grub, or a maggot. Caterpillars become moths or butterflies. Grubs turn into beetles, and maggots develop into flies."

Mr. Thomas circled the room, helping each of us identify our piles of collected items, and as he did so, he went on explaining:

"Complete metamorphosis is four stages, from egg to larva to **pupa** (PYOO-puh) and then to adult. Gradual metamorphosis usually means three stages: from egg to nymph to adult. The simplest growth pattern of all is that of scorpions and spiders, from egg to young to adult," Mr. Thomas told us.

"What is most important in order to complete the process of change," he said with emphasis, "is that the larva be kept warm, safe, dry, and well fed."

It seemed wonderfully simple to me. If I wanted my baby brother to change into a different form—a beetle or a fly—I must protect him from harm and see that he ate plenty of food and stayed warm and dry. Then, presto, no more baby brother.

My brain spun with possibilities. Would he turn into a june bug or a whirligig beetle? Would he live on land or in the irrigation ditch, or maybe the pond? I hardly knew where to begin in the making of my secret plans.

Mr. Thomas set me straight. When I started asking questions about how to turn human flesh into insect flesh, I gave myself away.

"Who is this individual you'd like to see changed into an insect?" he asked me one afternoon.

"My baby brother."

"He's small, yes?"

"He's three," I said. "Still in diapers."

"It's already too late," Mr. Thomas said, suppressing a smile. "He's already too human. Metamorphosis won't work."

I felt foolish, but I persisted a little, wanting more information than I was getting. "You said bees make a queen by what they feed the larvae, and you said worker ants can make more soldiers for their nest if they feed the larvae a certain kind of food, or more of it. Isn't that so?"

Mr. Thomas was gentle with me, and patient. "Yes," he said. "You are correct in these things. Think of it this way: Remember what I told you about spiders? How baby spiders are infinitely smaller than their mothers but nearly identical in every other respect?"

"Yes, I remember."

"This is the case with your baby brother. Although it may not seem so now, he is simply a small version of a grown-up man. Unfortunately, that is the fact of it. You'll have to accept it."

I did accept it, and Mr. Thomas improved my mood by giving me zoo duty. This meant it was my job to keep the animal captives fed and watered and to see to their bedding and nest material.

I was busy cleaning terrariums one afternoon, months later, when I saw a **chrysalis** (KRIS-uh-lis) break open right before my eyes.

Flakes of green casing—the pupal skin—split apart and fell away. Skinny black legs with hairs attached explored the air as if feeling for a way to go. A pair of wings unfolded slowly, gradually, and the most beautiful of butterflies appeared.

I watched as the butterfly adjusted its freshly exposed limbs and settled into a resting position, worn out from its effort. It takes a lot of energy to loosen a tight, skin covering and shed it once and for all.

The butterfly flew out the window, and I wondered if it might be headed for the mountain meadow where it had been discovered so many weeks earlier.

Changes in Physical Shape and Form

The precise moment of an insect's birth is hard to pin down. When a human baby is born, we know right away that it is human. An insect freshly hatched may be entirely different from its parent in appearance and every other respect.

Metamorphosis, the process that takes an insect from egg to adult, can be two, three, or four stages long. The number of stages depends on the species of insect.

Grasshoppers, earwigs, squash bugs, and stinkbugs are but a few of the insects that undergo three stages: egg, nymph (or larval stage), and adult. Dragonflies and mayflies, as well as stone flies, experience three stages as well: egg; **naiad** (NY-ad), which is an aquatic nymph, or larva; and adult.

Most moths, butterflies, bees, wasps, and ants experience the four stages of complete metamorphosis: egg, larva, pupa, and adult.

In their larval stages most insects are eating machines. Caterpillars, for example, eat and molt, or shed their skins, several times before entering the pupal stage. In their larval state insects are vulnerable to predators. Most are so carefully disguised, or camouflaged, they are extremely difficult to find.

When the larva has grown enough, it organizes into a pupa. It attaches itself to a safe, secure place—a leaf, rock, or spot of tree bark. Some insect larvae burrow into the ground.

When the pupal skin forms, the larval skin falls off. The new skin starts out soft and pliable, but it soon hardens. The firm covering is protection against bad weather and predators.

Dramatic change occurs inside the pupal skin. Each cell is transformed. What once was a caterpillar, a maggot, or a grub gradually becomes the adult of whatever species the insect belongs to. When the job is done, the adult wiggles its way out of the pupal skin and begins life anew.

The smaller the insect, the shorter its childhood. This is generally true. Strangely, there are moths that spend three times their life-span under the ground or beneath tree bark, existing as larvae. These animals spend just a matter of days as adults. Cicadas may stay underground anywhere from thirteen to seventeen years before hatching in such numbers that they make the air whine and whistle with their wings. Adult cicadas live only thirty to forty days.

EGGS AND LARVAL CASES

fly *(Diptera)*

butterfly *(Lepidoptera)*

beetle
(Coleoptera)

cockroach *(Blattodea)*

sweat bee
(Halictus zonulum)

ladybird beetle
(Coccinella novemnotata)

scarabaeid beetle
(Phanaeus vindex)

shot-hole borer
(bark beetle)
(Scolytus rugulosus)

ant lion
(Hesperolean abdominalis)

humpbacked fly
(Megaseolia scalaris)

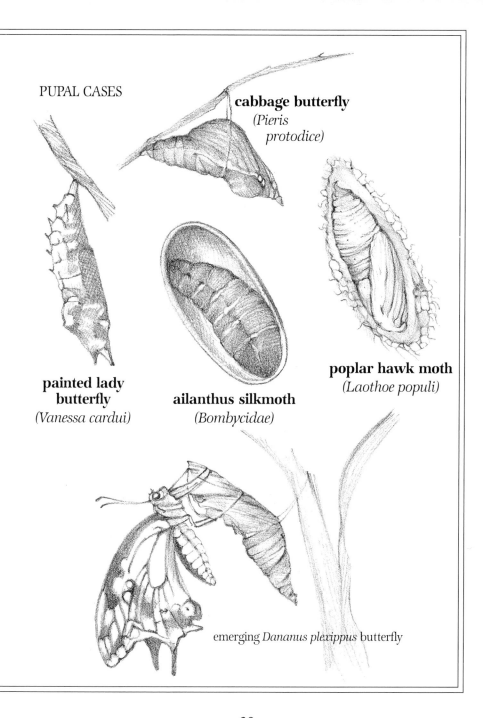

PUPAL CASES

cabbage butterfly
*(Pieris
protodice)*

poplar hawk moth
(Laothoe populi)

**painted lady
butterfly**
(Vanessa cardui)

ailanthus silkmoth
(Bombycidae)

emerging *Dananus plexippus* butterfly

Five

A WATERY NURSERY

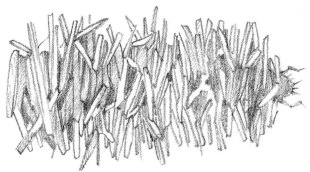

caddis fly larva inside its case   *scientific name: Oecetis cinerascens*

It was nearly spring and tadpole season. The pond smelled rotten and fresh at the same time. Martha and I had already spent long, wandering hours exploring the banks, keeping as still as statues to see what we might see by remaining motionless. We waited with uncommon patience for the velvet surface of the water to bubble and crease, a sure indication of tadpole presence.

We'd seen bundles of frog eggs hidden under leaves, their fragile interiors coated in a protective sheath of yellowish jelly. We knew that tadpoles were not going to be long in coming.

We wanted wild animals to raise. Unlike earthworms, tadpoles were not a cash crop. It was for the pure and simple love of it that we wanted to capture and grow them.

Finally we saw the telltale bubbles we'd been waiting for. They surged up between patches of drifting pond scum. Tadpoles were soon swarming. The pond water was bone-chilling cold, but we waded in with our jars and scooped up as many of the wiggly creatures as we could.

Martha got sixteen and I got eight.

We took the jars home and put them in a sunny window in my kitchen. Martha's mother fainted at the sight of slimy things and wouldn't have the jars in her house.

For three days we fed the tadpoles goldfish food I took from a supply my sisters kept for their pet goldfish. We observed our treasure with the guarded tenderness people exhibit when they watch lions or tigers. On the fourth day from the time we'd captured them, every tadpole was dead. Each one floated lifeless on the surface of the water in the jars.

We held a private funeral service, just Martha and I. We set the bodies alight and placed the remains on leaves we sent drifting across the pond. To urge the funeral rafts along, we poked them with willow sticks. While we were doing this we saw what tadpoles really like to eat. We had the answer to what we'd done wrong in caring for our wild animals.

In their natural state, tadpoles were swarming around bobbing strings of mosquito larvae—slim, pale beings clinging to the underside of the water surface.

"Our tadpoles died eating goldfish food," Martha said.

"Yeah," I agreed. "We gave them the wrong stuff to eat."

We lowered ourselves into the water so we could better see the myriad animals swimming about. Most were beetles with shiny black wing covers. Like the tadpoles, the beetles were snatching up the mosquito larvae.

That summer our days became oriented to water. We saw water boatmen swimming upside down, using their pair of long, fringed, oarlike legs to push with. Whirligig beetles spun on top of the water, traveling in bunches of six or seven. Their backs shone blue-black in the sunlight. The larvae of giant water beetles breathed air through hollow tubes built into their rear ends.

The deaths we caused by not knowing what to feed our tadpoles kept us from trying again. We satisfied our desire for closeness to wildness by pretending to be alligators drifting in the pond.

For hours on end we were able to see what we'd never seen before or even imagined.

41

Hatches of too-small-to-see (almost) midges and flies zipped and zoomed over the water or hung suspended in the air like puffs of smoke. Dragonflies met and mated and then flew in tandem searching for a place to lay eggs. Diving beetles the size of walnuts captured tadpoles and tiny, silvery fish too slow to get away.

After a while it was easy to see how life started in water. I wondered about the urge to speak, thinking it must have started in a wet place. Hearing the clicks, squeaks, croaks, and buzzes of countless aquatic creatures cast a spell on my brain. I wanted to learn their language, to whistle, whirr, and grumble.

We figured out that for some the pond is a dangerous place, where death comes quickly. For others the pond is a cradle, a nursery, where eggs float around until ready to hatch and larval insects creep on cool bottom mud.

One day Martha and I slid into the water in our usual clothing— tee-shirts, shorts, and no shoes. Suddenly Martha let out a howl loud enough to scare the birds out of the trees. "I've stepped on something!" she screamed. "Something horrible!"

It turned out to be a mud puppy, a harmless salamander with yellow stripes on its black skin. After this incident Martha was less keen on being a pretend alligator. We took to walking along the river every day, where an entirely new set of experiences with wildness awaited us.

At Home in the Water

It's hard to figure out what it would feel like to be at home in the water, to live with gills, breathing tubes, bubbles attached to your rear end, and constantly on the alert for a hungry dragonfly nymph out to get you.

Aquatic insects that dwell full time in water have adapted special body parts to allow them this watery existence. Diving beetles have legs shaped like oars. Their backs and bellies are rounded and streamlined for swift movement through the element they live in. Many water beetles breathe through special tubes attached to their bodies. Other beetles in wet places have hairs on their backsides that collect air at the surface, forming bubbles that become an underwater air supply when the beetles dive.

Millions of pond, stream, lake, and river insects are in the environment temporarily. They move on to land or air once grown. Mayfly nymphs spend a year in fast-rushing water. At hatching time they surge to the surface and climb up plant stems. There they flex their new muscles and break their nymphal skins to emerge as airborne adults.

Caddis flies are easy-to-find residents of ponds and streams. Many of them cover their tender, soft parts with tiny "houses" made of pebbles, leaf bits, and mud, held together with saliva.

Insects in larval forms often produce silk and use it in remarkable ways. A species of caddis fly in its larval stage spins a silken underwater net that stretches from one rock to another. This web catches fragments of dead plants and animals, which the caddis fly eats.

One major predator in any pond or lake is the dragonfly nymph. With powerful jaws, a lower lip that extends for grabbing prey, and a seemingly endless appetite, this agile beast eats anything it can catch, from tadpoles to insect larvae to small fish.

You will see all sorts of aquatic insects just by watching the surface of the water. Water striders zip around, the surface acting as a floor for their feet to run on. Hairs covering their bodies capture air, so it is impossible for these animals to sink.

Mosquito larvae are often called "wigglers." They cling to the underside of the water and wiggle from side to side whenever the water moves. They breathe air through tubes built into their heads. Many wigglers are devoured by a variety of pond animals, but enough survive to create clouds of obnoxious biters on a summer evening.

Healthy lakes, streams, and ponds have a great wealth of insect life, from the muddy or sandy bottoms to the glassy surfaces pricked with pond weeds and floating leaves. The diversity of life is perhaps more clear in a watery place than anywhere else on earth.

Types of Mosquitoes and Flies

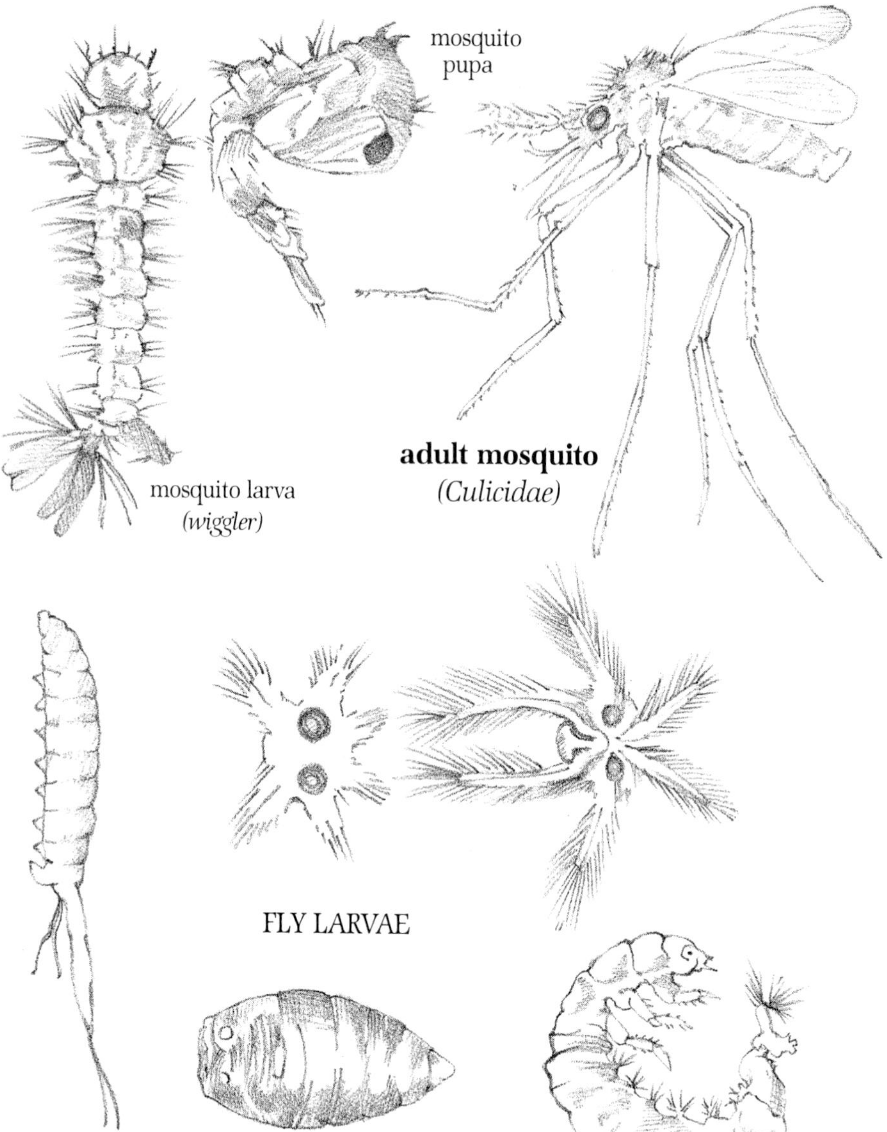

mosquito
pupa

mosquito larva
(wiggler)

adult mosquito
(Culicidae)

FLY LARVAE

44

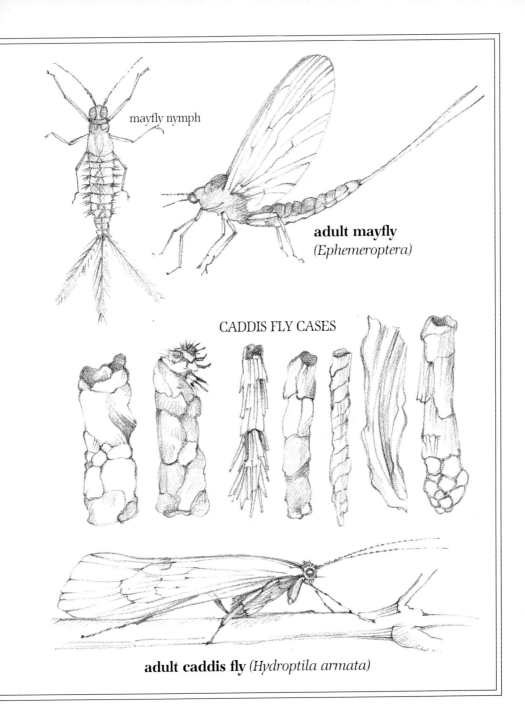

mayfly nymph

adult mayfly
(Ephemeroptera)

CADDIS FLY CASES

adult caddis fly *(Hydroptila armata)*

Six

THE TRUTH ABOUT BLACK WIDOW SPIDERS

black widow spider   *scientific name: Latrodectus mactans*

There is no worse fate, no more gruesome bad luck, than to be bitten by a black widow spider. This was the firmly held opinion of everybody I knew when I was growing up. It wasn't just kids who believed this; it was adults, too.

We knew that a black widow bite meant death would follow, but only after a prolonged period of terrible suffering, of boils and ulcers that wept green pus, and of drastic swelling of the arms and legs.

We lived in a spidery world, a rural environment where multi-legged, segmented animals crossed our paths daily. No spider had the chilling effect on our imaginations that the black widow had. The truth about these spiders remained a mystery until a cousin came from Chicago to spend the summer.

She was my age, which was eight at the time. She slept in my room during her stay. "She's the same age as you," my mother explained. "She'll be your playmate this summer."

I didn't mind Niki's sharing my room until I found out she snored. Her snores were the kind that went on all night long and kept even the soundest sleeper (me) wide awake.

I was afraid to say anything, until one morning when I couldn't stay awake at the breakfast table. "I'm sleeping out tonight," I announced, expecting an argument. None came.

"Me, too," Niki said.

I hadn't bargained on Niki's joining me. She was too civilized, too orderly, neat, and prim to want to brave it on the ground in a sleeping bag. It was her first trip West. She was afraid of everything, from wading in the ditch to climbing hay bales in the barn.

"You'll be scared," I said. "You won't like it. Things crawl around in the night and make sounds. You'll hate it."

"Now, now," my mother said, overhearing us, "Niki can do as she likes, and you will take care of her."

I was stuck. That same night we slept out under a starry sky next to a flower bed thick with hollyhock stalks.

It was one of Niki's better nights when it came to snoring. I slept well and woke up before she did, in that stillness of first light that is still one of my favorite times of day.

I sat up and rubbed my eyes and then looked over at Niki, who was half out of her sleeping bag. I saw a small red swelling on her wrist. It had a white dot in the middle of it. It was a bite, and it hadn't been there when we'd gone to sleep.

I stared at the bite and realized I'd never seen one quite like it. My sisters and brother and I had been stung and bitten by bees, wasps, hornets, and ants. I knew what the results of these stabs to the skin looked like, and Niki's bite was different.

By the time we were eating breakfast, Niki's arm was swollen to the elbow. The white dot was the size of a quarter, and the skin around it was purple.

"What happened to your arm?" my mother asked.

"I got bitten," Niki said, tears welling in her pale blue eyes. "Something bit me while we slept out."

"Looks like a spider bite," my father said. "Did you bite the beast back?"

"It's not funny," I said. I was familiar with my father's teasing ways, but Niki wasn't.

"Is it painful?" my mother asked. "Here, let me see it close up." She reached for Niki's arm.

"Ouch!" Niki cried. "It hurts!"

"This is serious," my mother said, watching Niki twist away, protecting her hurt arm with her good one. "I think we'd better take Niki into town and have the doctor check this out."

My father protested. We rarely went to town to see the doctor. We were expected to cure ourselves. It was because Niki was a cousin, and not one of us, that he gave in.

On the way to town, twenty-six miles away, Niki got worse. She was dizzy and had to throw up, so we stopped by the side of the road.

In my heart of hearts I knew what had happened to Niki, and I knew I was responsible. Black widow spiders had webs in the tangled mass of hollyhocks near where we'd slept. She would be dead in a matter of days, the victim of a black widow. I could say nothing. It was too horrible, and it was my fault. If I'd been tolerant of her snoring, we'd have stayed inside and she would still be fine.

The doctor examined Niki, and he let my mother and me stay and watch. "A black widow spider bite," he said. "I've seen these before. She'll recover, but she's having a severe reaction to the venom."

"She'll recover?" I asked "She'll be okay? Are you sure? How do you know?"

"People rarely die of these bites," the doctor said, smiling at me kindly.

I looked at Niki's arm, now swollen to the shoulder. I wanted to believe the doctor. I wanted to know that Niki would get better, grow up, get married, and have children the same as most people do.

Niki did get better, but it took her four days of staying in bed and missing meals. I stayed with her, reading stories and putting cold cloths on her forehead. I told her I was sorry for what I'd done. I told her the whole thing was my doing.

"No," Niki said. "It wasn't your fault." She sounded surprised by my confession. "I know I snore. My sisters told me. I wanted to sleep out. You didn't make me. I wanted to be your friend and do what you do. I didn't want to be chicken."

"You're not chicken," I said, filled with admiration at the way Niki had dealt with her spider bite. "I think you're brave."

Niki was now a neighborhood celebrity, famous for surviving what was supposed to be a fatal experience. Even my sisters came to view the greenish **ulcer** (UL-sir) that formed once the swelling went down. "Is that going to spread all over your body?" one of my sisters asked.

"No," Niki said, grinning. I could see she was thinking about fooling the two doubting older girls, telling them a tale of limbs dropping off and putrefied flesh. "The doctor said I'll be good as new once the ulcer heals."

Since that time I've realized that spiders, even black widows, hardly ever kill people. Our terror of these animals is fifty times more potent than any venom they might inject into our bodies.

Spiders and Venom

The venom a black widow spider makes is one of the strongest toxins in the animal kingdom. Still, its harmful effects are rarely experienced by humans. The venom delivered by North America's other most feared spider, the brown recluse or violin spider, is just as potent. This spider, too, is rarely responsible for human death.

It is the particular chemical mix of venom that makes it dangerous. In human victims the skin around the fang mark dies, creating an ulcer that takes time to heal. The victim may feel nausea and weakness for a few days, but in time all symptoms pass.

Spiders use their venom to paralyze insect prey that they snare in webs or that they stalk and capture. Venom acts as a digestive juice. Once inside the prey animal, the venom breaks down the intestines and other organs into fluids that the spider drains out.

Spiders are arachnids, members of the class Arachnida, which

Types of Spiders

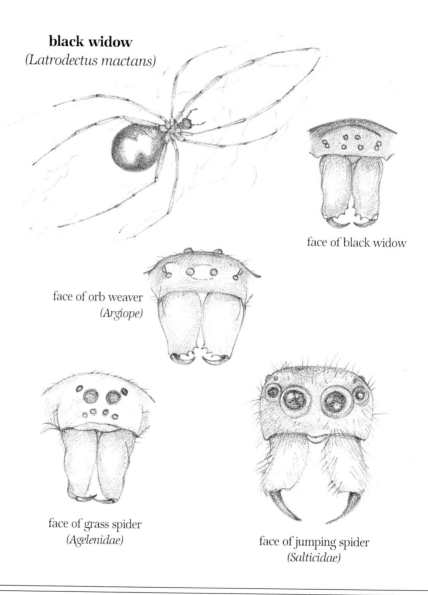

black widow
(Latrodectus mactans)

face of black widow

face of orb weaver
(Argiope)

face of grass spider
(Agelenidae)

face of jumping spider
(Salticidae)

black widow in her web

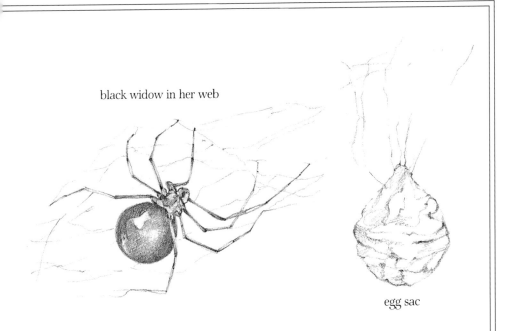

egg sac

BODY OF A SPIDER

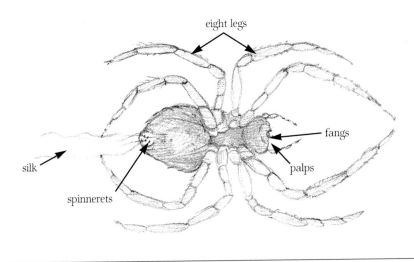

eight legs

fangs

palps

silk

spinnerets

includes ticks, mites, and scorpions. These creatures began to evolve hundreds of millions of years ago. The oldest-known scorpion fossil dates from four hundred million years ago.

Spiders are different from insects because they have eight legs, not six, and two main body parts, not three. In addition, spiders make silk all their lives. Certain species of insects do make silk, but only in their larval stages.

Spiders use silk as nets, webs, snares, traps, burrow linings, and draglines. Spiders wrap paralyzed prey in silk shrouds and build durable egg sacs for their eggs out of many layers of silk woven together.

Silk is made in glands in the rear of a spider's body. It leaves the spider through tiny spigots in organs called **spinnerets** (spin-uh-RET). A spider can open or close its spigots as needed. Some spiders make seven different kinds of silk, but most make four or five. Spider silk is one of the strongest known fibers on earth, as elastic as rubber, even stronger than steel wire of the same size.

Spiders are carnivorous and eat meat. Web builders, such as the black widow, spin a web and live in it their entire lives, patching and mending when needed. Web builders usually die once their eggs are laid and wrapped in sacs the spider safely stows away.

Spiders that do not spin permanent webs are called wandering spiders. They are always on the move, searching for and capturing prey. Spiders, like insects, have evolved remarkable ways to survive. They can be frozen, and once thawed, they return to normal immediately. Spiders live underwater, spinning silk nurseries that they fill with air, trapped in hairs on their backsides, brought down from the surface. Spiders live on Mount Everest and in the hottest deserts. One way or another, spiders find ways to make do.

Spiders are shy. Even the black widow would rather escape than be forced to sink her fangs into an intruder in her web, unless it is a potential meal. However, most spiders, no matter how reclusive, will strike in self-defense.

Seven

SUMMER INVASIONS

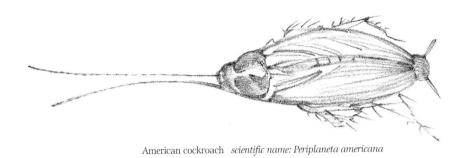

American cockroach *scientific name: Periplaneta americana*

 On a summer afternoon when I was ten, my mother asked me to ride my bike to the store and pick up some things for her.

"You can put them in your bicycle basket to get them home," she said.

I set off up the dirt road, going slowly because it was a hot day and it didn't do to hurry in the heat.

On summer days I was used to hearing the noises of insects all around—on the ground, in the trees, in the air—unseen but loud. This day I heard something else: a throbbing sound that came heavily to my ears. It was not a gentle hum; it was deeper and more persistent. It was getting nearer every second.

At the store I got the things on my mother's list and headed for the door.

"Watch out for those locusts," the store owner said as I let the screen door bang behind me. "I hear it's quite a swarm coming this way."

I didn't pay much attention, thinking I wasn't sure what a locust looked like. Was it the same as a grasshopper?

I stuffed the groceries into my basket and turned for home. In less than a quarter mile the beat of sound I'd heard before became a thunderous roar. I felt the stinging pop of winged insects hitting my bare arms and the back of my neck.

I nearly lost control of the bike, trying to pull off the road so I could look behind me, in the direction the insects were coming from.

The sky above the trees was smoky-brown, darkened by the hugeness of the swarm. They landed on me, becoming tangled in my braids. They clung to my pant legs and covered the metal frame of my bike as if determined to devour it.

They looked like grasshoppers, only darker and bigger than any I'd ever seen before. They crawled and crept and flew across the valley, traveling from the northeast toward the southwest, chomping on any growing thing.

When I got home that day and tore into the kitchen through the back door, my mother was waiting, her eyes wide with fear. Immediately she began plucking locusts off my body.

My family sat around in the kitchen for hours, waiting for the swarm of locusts to pass. When we went outside, the air was still, as if the earth had stopped spinning.

There were heaps of dead and dying locusts on the ground. My father, ever one to despise insects, ordered us to help rake the creatures into piles. He set these on fire.

I hated the sight and smell of the burning locusts, but there was nothing else to do to be rid of the bodies, and I knew this.

That summer we had two more invasions. One was especially hard for me because I was in charge of the cleanup. Tent caterpillars, the larval form of a moth, infested our cottonwood trees.

"You like to climb trees," my father said, fixing me with his eyes. "I want you to get up there and pull those nests out."

I did as I was told and it was awful work.

Tent caterpillars spin silk out of their mouths. They construct sticky, complicated webs that surround their colonies. There seemed to

54

be millions of them collected together in the cottonwood trees, stripping the leaves to nothing.

With gloved hands I tugged at the webbing. Caterpillars got stuck on my skin and fell like greenish-brown rain around my face. If I tried to pick one off myself, it broke and stained my fingers with caterpillar innards. When the job was finally done, it was weeks before I no longer dreamed of caterpillars.

The final invasion that summer was one of cockroaches in the house. There were so many that when we came in after dark and switched on a light we could hear the thumping of countless cockroach feet as the insects ran for cover.

My mother nearly killed the family by using a powder form of pesticide that she placed in cups on lamps left lit all night. Heat turned the powder into a gas. We developed headaches and stomachaches before realizing we were slowly dying, while the cockroaches were doing fine.

Cockroaches are famous for their survival skills. They put other insects to shame with their appetites for just about anything and with their repro- ductive efficiency. The cockroach is a "living fossil," meaning a species of cockroach very much like what we see today existed on Earth four hundred million years ago. The cock- roaches of primeval times would have created an even greater dilemma for my mother than the ones we had. In those long-ago times cockroaches were the size of small house cats.

Back then I had no idea why locusts swarmed, and I could only speculate on why tent caterpillars lived in gluey masses in the treetops. I wondered why the cockroaches chose our house and not the neigh- bor's. I decided insects have secret agendas humans cannot understand.

I still quake at the thought of being surrounded in a mass of flying insects. I think it's a natural and innate fear we all have.

Migratory Grasshopper

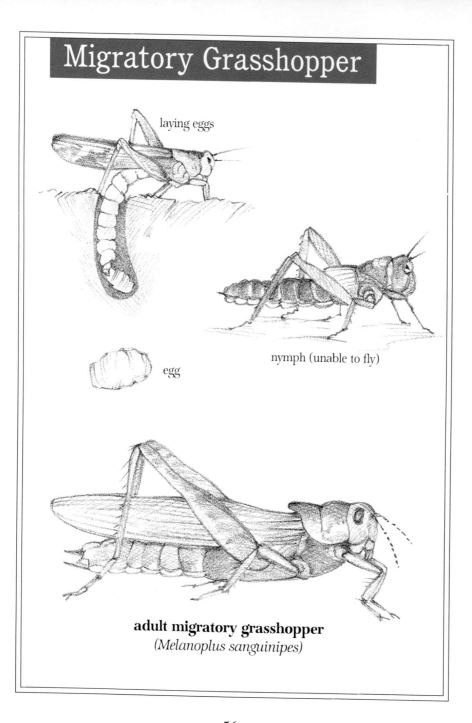

laying eggs

nymph (unable to fly)

egg

adult migratory grasshopper
(Melanoplus sanguinipes)

Eastern Tent Caterpillar

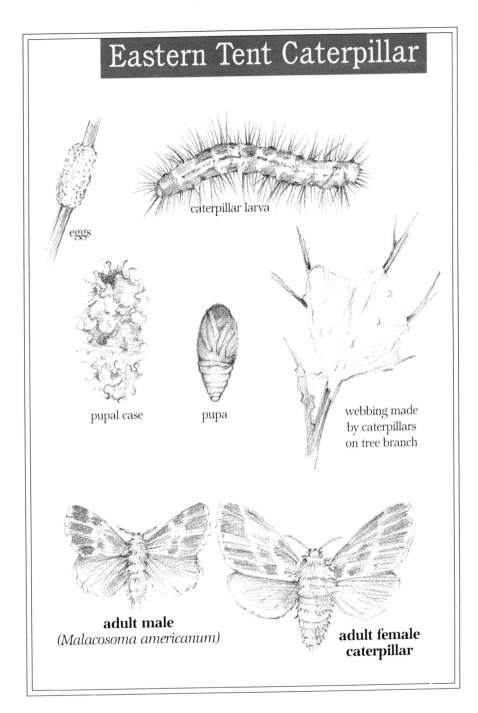

eggs

caterpillar larva

pupal case

pupa

webbing made
by caterpillars
on tree branch

adult male
(Malacosoma americanum)

**adult female
caterpillar**

Swarms and Hordes

Reasons for insects swarming and gathering in huge numbers vary according to which insect species is involved. Social insects function in perfect harmony, almost like one single organism. The tent caterpillars that so upset me as a child were doing what insect larvae always do: they were eating and staying safe until the time came for their transformation into moths.

Some insect species may **migrate** (MY-grate), traveling long distances, because seasonal changes, warmer or colder temperatures, and increasing or diminishing light drive them.

Perhaps the best-known migratory insect is the monarch butterfly. Huge flocks of these fragile insects travel hundreds of miles south to winter in Mexican forests, only to return north again in the spring. Changes in temperature and light set these butterflies in motion.

Most grasshoppers become migratory in response to seasonal changes, but some migrations are triggered by overpopulation and hunger.

At times grasshoppers hatch out in such numbers that their home range cannot support them. As they grow, their bodies produce extra-high levels of hormones that hasten their development. In less time than it takes an ordinary grasshopper to become an adult, these migratory locusts grow wings and take to the air.

Their flights take them great distances, and when they come down to earth, they devour whatever living crop they find.

Since the beginning of human agriculture, migratory locusts have done terrible damage to human food supplies, though some people capture and eat locusts. Once swarms are under way, it is impossible to halt them. One must take shelter and wait until the swarm has passed.

Conclusion

THE BACKGROUND MUSIC OF CHILDHOOD

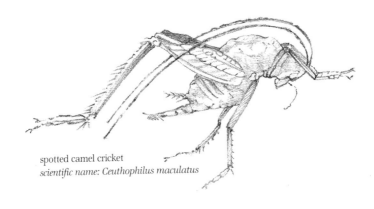

spotted camel cricket
scientific name: Ceuthophilus maculatus

One of my sisters said, "What's making that sound?"

My other sister answered, "Crickets."

"How do they make that sound?" I asked.

One sister said, "With their voices, silly. Don't you know anything?"

"You're wrong," my other sister said. "Crickets rub their legs together to make their noises."

"How do you know?" I asked, believing her but wondering how she knew.

"I watched one time," my sister said. "If you can get close enough, the cricket kind of forgets you're there. Then you can see the legs rubbing together."

"How come they do it?" I asked. "Do you know that?"

"Maybe it's to talk to each other in the dark," my sister answered. "Like we're doing now."

Our conversation about cricket sounds happened one night when

59

the moon was full and rising. We'd gotten permission to go down to the river, to lie on the sand and listen to the sounds of the night.

cricket *(Orthoptera)*

There were always sounds to hear.

Insect songs were the background music of my childhood. If there had come a silence in the space around my ears, I'd have decided the world had ended.

We lived up the river from an Indian pueblo. When the Indians held dances, we could hear the beat of their drums. Sometimes I'd be sitting by the pond, under the willows, or in the irrigation ditch cooling off, and the drum rhythms would come through the branches and leaves of the willows, through the trees. The drum noises would gradually merge with the buzzes, whirrs, and hummings of insects.

I'd close my eyes and the sounds would flow through my brain like water sloshing in a bowl. Each smooth, low throb of a drum met an insect signal, and the two became one.

The harmony of it stayed with me. It seems we're all a part of that other world, the insect world, and they are a part of our world. We forget that most of the time. When we remember it, that is when we hear the music in our ears.

GLOSSARY

abdomen (AB-doe-men) The third and rear part of an insect's body. The abdomen is attached to the thorax, and during an insect's adult stage it bears no legs.

amber (AM-ber) Fossilized sap, or resin. Amber is hard, yellowish material that is sometimes polished and used in jewelry.

antenna (an-TEN-uh); *plural:* antennae (an-TEN-ee) One of a pair of slender, movable, segmented sensory organs on the head of insects.

cannibal (KAN-i-bul) A person who eats human flesh; any animal that eats its own kind.

carnivore (KARN-i-vor) Any species that feeds on animal tissue. *See* vegetarian

chitin (KITE-in) A tough, horny material that forms most of the hard outer covering of insects and crabs.

chrysalis (KRIS-uh-lis) A pupa of a butterfly; any insect pupa. *See* pupa

entomologist (en-tuh-MALL-uh-jist) Someone who deals in the study of insects is an entomologist. This scientific discipline is called entomology.

enzyme (EN-zime) A substance similar to protein in plant and animal cells. Enzymes are chemicals that work to speed up or slow down reactions and responses in organisms.

fangs (FANGZ) Long slender "teeth" embedded in a spider's jaws. Fangs have ducts inside through which venom flows. The fangs pierce the prey and are part of the delivery system for the venom.

fumigate (FEW-muh-gate) To fumigate is to expose to gas, fumes, or smoke for the purpose of exterminating or killing.

infested (in-FEST-ed) To be overrun. An infested area is invaded by such large numbers of animals that the situation becomes bothersome or dangerous.

insect (IN-sekt) Any of a class of arthropods with well-defined head, thorax, and abdomen, only three pairs of legs, and typically one or two pairs of wings.

larva (LAR-vuh), *plural:* larvae (LAR-vee) The development, or growing stage, between egg and adult insect.

mammal (MAM-ul) Any of a group of warm-blooded animals that nourish their young with milk from mammary glands, skin is usually covered with hair, and include humans.

mandible (MAN-di-bul) The upper and lower jaws on an insect, toothed in chewing types and sharply pointed, hollow, or grooved in sucking types.

metamorphosis (met-uh-MORE-foh-sis) A more or less abrupt developmental change in the form or structure of an animal occurring after birth or hatching.

migrate (MY-grate) To move from one place or locality to another.

naiad (NY-ad) The young of a dragonfly, damselfly, mayfly, or stone fly when it is in its aquatic stage.

nocturnal (nock-TER-nul) Active at night.

nymph (NIMF) An immature form of any insect that experiences incomplete metamorphosis, such as a grasshopper.

palps (POWLPS) Jointed organs or feelers for touching and tasting, attached to the mouthparts of insects and spiders.

parasite (PAIR-uh-site) An animal that has to live off another in order to survive. Parasites differ from predators in that they require a single "host" to ensure their survival. *See* predator

predator (PRED-uh-tore) An animal that gets its food by the killing and consuming of other animals.

protein (PRO-teen) Any of a large number of substances that are the union of elements such as oxygen and nitrogen. Proteins are essential in the diets of animals. Proteins exist in all plant and animal matter on Earth.

pupa (PYOO-puh) The inactive stage of an insect's life during which it transforms into an adult.

spinneret (spin-uh-RET) The organ in the rear of a spider's body, on the abdomen, through which silk passes from the inside of the spider to the outside.

terrarium (teh-RARE-ee-um) A container, usually made of glass, set up with soil, rocks, and plants and used to hold land animals. Terrariums are ideal for keeping animals while observing them.

thorax (THOR-aks) The midsection of an insect's body, which bears the legs and wings.

toxin (TOCK-sin) A poisonous substance that is made by a living organism, such as an insect, and is toxic, sometimes deadly, when introduced into the tissues of another organism.

translucent (trans-LOO-cent) A material that light can pass through but objects beyond cannot be seen clearly.

ulcer (UL-sir) An open sore, not a wound, that may be inside or outside the body. Ulcers fester and drip pus as living tissue dies.

vegetarian (vej-eh-TAIR-ee-un) People who refuse to eat meat, for a variety of reasons. People or animals who subsist on a diet of vegetables only. *See* carnivore

venom (VEN-um) A juice, or poison, produced inside the bodies of some spiders and snakes and introduced into a prey animal through a bite or sting.

vermin (VERM-in) Small, common, harmful or objectionable animals (as lice or fleas) that are difficult to control.

INDEX